Loving G

Loving God, Loving You

Marion Stroud

Pickering Paperbacks

First published 1973 under the title "I Love God and You" by Falcon Books

This edition published 1985

by Pickering & Inglis,
3 Beggarwood Lane,
Basingstoke, Hants RG23 7LP,
United Kingdom

British Library CIP Data

Stroud, Marion
Loving God, loving you.—2nd ed.
1. Women—Religious life
I. Title II. Stroud, Marion. I love God and you
248.8′43 BV4527

ISBN 0-7208-0633-X

Reproduced, printed and bound in Great Britain by
Hazell Watson & Viney Limited,
Member of the BPCC Group,
Aylesbury, Bucks

Contents

Foreword

Sometimes I find myself being asked to speak to a women's group about my own personal faith in Jesus Christ and the difference this faith has made in my life. Two questions nearly always raised are: 'How did your husband react to your becoming a Christian?' and/or 'Don't you think it can cause a lot of trouble between a husband and wife when one is a committed Christian and the other is not?'

When these questions are asked the wife is usually voicing the fears of others present besides herself, and I have a real responsibility to answer her truthfully and at length when time allows. But there are difficulties.

When I learned that Marion Stroud was writing a book that would have these two questions uppermost in mind, I was impatient to see it; having done so, I thank God for the wisdom and courage He gave her in bringing it to completion. I feel it is a must for any woman, of any age, who would dare, or has dared, to put God first in her life and, as a result, fears for its effect upon her marriage and family life. Having trod this tight-rope for several years until my husband, in spite of me, became a Christian, I can only wish it had been available earlier; now that it is I shall use it and recommend it strongly to others.

Mrs Stroud has researched among a wide selection of Christian women and this book identifies with and understands their frustrations, heartaches and sometimes loneliness. It is wonderfully practical and realistic, pointing always to the One who has been her inspiration.

R. JACOBS

1 *Let's start at the very beginning*

If you are perfectly content with your life as it is and feel no need of any help outside yourself, then this book is not for you.

If you have never wondered what life is all about, or wished that you could unravel the tangle of the past and start afresh, then read no further than this. You see, God's offer of forgiveness and a purposeful, loving relationship with Himself can only be appreciated or accepted by those with a sense of need.

Take Jane for example. Jane first began to notice that life has its problems when she was fifteen or so. Her mother put her moodiness down to her age; her father reckoned that it was the worry of exams. Jane knew that they were both wrong – about that as about everything else. Once she got away from the confines of home and school she was certain that all her troubles would be over.

Certainly, the freedom of a job in London, and the flat which she shared there was exhilarating at first, but all too soon the pressures started to build up, as one by one her friends began to flaunt their engagement rings. Freedom to do her own thing, no longer seemed so very desirable.

However, before life could get too grey and dreary along came Peter, and Jane heaved a sigh of relief. She was not on the shelf after all! Soon she was engaged, then married with a dear little flat; surely everything would be perfect now. And so it was . . . for a little while.

But of course the dear little flat was only a temporary measure whilst they saved up for a deposit on the house. Having moved in, Jane just could not wait to give up her job – both her neighbours were pushing very new and shiny prams!

Jane had her babies and gained more than she had bargained for. She was rather shattered to realize that to be the ideal wife and mother so glowingly portrayed in women's magazines required more than the possession of husband and children! There were the good days of course, but on the others, when life seemed to be one long round of tidying toys and answering the same question for the sixtieth time, Jane decided that what she really needed was a job. It would be an outside interest, to stretch her mind and spread a little jam on life's dreary bread and butter.

At last the children were at school, and Jane found just the job that she wanted. She had reached her goal, but still that elusive butterfly of perfect happiness fluttered just one step ahead.

Like most of us, Jane was not very anxious to admit her dissatisfaction to anyone. For years she had been living in the future; reaching out for the next stage in life; certain that this would complete her happiness. But things had not turned out as she had intended.

Instead of being the perfect patient mother to clean, tidy and obedient children, she found herself shouting impatiently at untidy, self-willed little beings, who often compared her unfavourably with their teacher. She knew that many of her friends envied her happy marriage and interesting job, and yet this bed of roses was not without its thorns. Even with Peter there were some things that she could not share; an inner loneliness and restlessness that it seemed disloyal and ungrateful to admit.

It was then that Jane paused for a moment to think things out. What was the point of all this frantic activity? She had everything that was supposed to make life complete, and nothing that gave her the key to life itself. She took a good look at herself – and looked away again quickly. She had to admit that the trouble stemmed from inside herself, because people and circumstances changed things very little. So for months Jane tried to exercise her will-power and change herself. It was not a success. Nothing altered: the restlessness and dissatisfaction were still there and got worse as time went on. Eventually she stopped trying and had to admit defeat, and it was then, having reached rock-bottom, that Jane was ready to meet the one person who could transform her life – Jesus Christ.

We all have different goals in life and various ways of achieving them. Like Jane, many of us spend long years thinking that final satisfaction is just around the corner, and then find that we have been chasing rainbows after all. But there is good news for all rainbow-chasers. God loves individual men and women and offers the wonderful gift of a fresh start and a new life to everyone – on condition that we admit our need. Of course, we all hate having to admit that we have needs that we cannot cope with, and yet this is essential before those needs can be met. So having faced up to that point, let's see how this change from the old life to the new can come about.

The background to it all

In the beginning God created men and women so that they would live in a happy and loving relationship with Himself; a two-way traffic of love flowing between them. But because God did not want mere machines that did all the right things automatically, He gave people the ability to choose – between good and evil, between going their own way or God's way. And men and women chose to go their own way. Thinking that they knew best, they decided to live as they pleased, and ignore God's claims on their lives. It was not long before they discovered that life away from God was only half a life, but by then it was too late. The rebellion had started that has affected people all the way down through history.

The Bible calls this turning our back on God 'sin', and sin has formed a barrier between God and us, cutting us off from the kind of life, in touch with Himself, that God wants us to have. It makes no difference whether we have pleased ourselves rather than God in one part of our lives or in everything, the sin barrier exists for everyone. We cannot tunnel our way through it by our good resolutions, kind deeds or an outward show of religion. It is a blight on our lives, and we are stuck with it.

The next move had to be from God's side. Loving people as He does, He longed to set us free from the chains of our own making, and yet being wholly just, He could not ignore the sin barrier. It had to be dealt with. Someone had to pay to have it removed. So Jesus came – God himself in a human body; the perfect link between the two sides.

Jesus Christ was completely human. He knew what it was to work hard with His hands in a land occupied by enemy forces. He had few material possessions and no settled home life. He knew what it meant to be hungry, tired, and hounded by men who hated Him. Yet in spite of these outward circumstances, He showed how life is meant to be lived; full of love, joy, peace and a freedom which nothing could destroy. Having lived a life that pleased God the Father in every respect, He allowed Himself to be crucified, the innocent willingly accepting the death penalty passed on the guilty. But the story does not end there. Death could not hold the Son of God captive. After three days He was more alive than ever, and is still alive today. So God Himself did what we could not do. He paid the price and dealt with the barrier between us.

Now His gift of a past forgotten and a present full of joy, purpose and freedom to live as God intends, is available to everyone. God longs for us to accept this gift, but He does not promise that our acceptance will insure us against all life's problems and difficulties. Nor will it turn us into perfect people overnight. What He does promise is His help and company in every circumstance, and His power within our very beings to change us just as much as we will allow Him to do.

So far, we have seen that all the activity has come from God's side. The new life and the fresh start are available as a free gift but it is not ours until we take it. In our household, special offer and free gift leaflets flutter through the letter box at least once a week. But they have no value at all to me, unless I take them to the appropriate shop and claim what is being offered. So how do we make the gift that

God offers, our own personal property? Let's take it step by step.

1 We *admit* that we have sinned and that there is nothing that we can do to change ourselves.
2 We *believe* that Jesus took our punishment, and that through what He has done alone, the barrier between God and ourselves has been removed.
3 We *turn away* from our old attitudes, telling God that we are sorry for our wrong-doing and thinking, and asking for His forgiveness.
4 We *hand over* the control of our life to Jesus Christ, thanking Him for all that He did to make this fresh start possible, and asking Him to live out His life through us.

If you are ready to do this, perhaps you would like to pray this prayer, and start right now on the biggest adventure that life has to offer.

'Lord Jesus I know that my life has fallen short of Your standards and that I am out of touch with You. I cannot change myself. I believe that You took the punishment that I deserve, so that I can be forgiven and changed. Thank You for loving me so much. I am truly sorry for the past; please take over the controls of my life, and make me into the kind of person that You want me to be.'

2 *Living and learning*

So now you have been adopted! That is, if you have prayed the prayer in chapter one, and meant it. The Bible says that when you become a Christian, you are adopted into the Christian family. God is your Father; you can share all your joys and problems with Him, and He can be trusted to care for your every need. Every other man or woman who has committed his or her life to Jesus Christ has a special relationship with you – the Bible calls it being 'brothers and sisters in the Lord'. As in any other family, its members do not always see eye to eye about things, and they may have totally different personalities and abilities. Nevertheless, whether they come from the South Sea Islands or Swindon, Birmingham or Borneo, Christians have one all-important thing in common. They have all come into the family in the same way – through trusting Jesus Christ as their Saviour.

And not only do you have a new and enormous family, but you yourself are a new person. The Bible says so. 'If any one is in Christ, he is a new creation; the old has passed away, behold, the new has come' (2 Corinthians 5.17).

Now this is a statement of fact, and as such is true, whether you *feel* that it is or not. People's reactions to becoming a Christian vary tremendously. Some folk really do feel 'new all over', and know immediately and with absolute certainty that their life has taken a complete about turn. Others *feel* no different at first, and can easily wonder if anything has happened to them at all. That is, if they rely upon *feelings*. But to *rely* on feelings is unnecessary and can be dangerous. Does this mean that feelings do not count at all? Of course not. God has given us our emotions and He wants us to feel His love and friendship. This is one of the reasons why Jesus Christ gives every new Christian His gift of the Holy Spirit to live within their very personality. He reassures us that we are really God's children. The Bible says, 'It is the Spirit himself bearing witness with our spirit that we are children of God' (Romans 8.16).

However, feelings should not be the foundation of your faith. As we all know, feelings can vary with the day of the week, the behaviour of our nearest and dearest and the state of our hormones – to mention just a few factors! So how can you *know* that you are a Christian; that the past is forgiven and forgotten, and that Jesus Christ is always with you, moment by moment through the most humdrum day? You can know it because God says so in the Bible. Trust His promises; unlike your feelings they do not change.

So on the days when you are one of the 'not sure' brigade, make use of these verses from the Bible. They are like rocks that you can fling at the demons of doubt.

John 3.16 'For God so loved the world (which includes you) that He gave His only Son, that whoever believes in Him should not perish but have eternal life.'

Revelation 3.20 'Behold I stand at the door and

knock; if anyone hears my voice and opens the door, I will come in.'

God loves you: if you have believed and opened the door of your life to Jesus, then you *are* a Christian and you have God's gift of eternal life.

Many verses from the Bible assure us that God will forgive our wrongdoing. Here are some from the Old Testament.

Psalm 103.10, 12 'He does not deal with us according to our sins or requite us according to our iniquities.

'As far as the east is from the west, so far does He remove our transgressions from us.'

So, with the mistakes of the past put so far behind you, you can enjoy the company of Jesus Christ day by day. It does not matter that you cannot see Him or hear Him speaking audibly; you have His promise, 'Lo, I am with you always, to the close of the age' (Matthew 28.20).

So much for knowing that you are a new person and safely within the Christian family. What happens next? Well, you start to grow up! And just as a baby needs the right sort of food to enable him to grow, so the new Christian has to make use of the food that God has given in the Bible. Neglect the Bible and you will stay a baby Christian all your life.

Where do you start?

You have taken the family Bible down off the shelf and blown the dust off its covers – now what do you do? One thing that you do not do is to start at the beginning of Genesis and aim to plod right through to the end of Revelation. The Bible is not just one book; it is a complete library of 66 books within one cover. And just as you do not present a new baby with 'roast beef and two veg.' for dinner, so the new Christian needs to start with 'the milk of the word'. Time enough to tackle the difficult books when you have grown some spiritual teeth.

But before we consider which parts of the Bible to read, let's think of which version of the Bible you should read them from. If you have a Bible at all, it is probably the Authorised Version, well-known, trusted and loved, but terribly hard to follow in places. Nowadays there are so many paraphrases and modern translations available that there is no need to be stuck with something that you cannot understand. The Revised Standard Version is similar enough to the Authorised Version for you to feel at home, and yet is more modern and understandable. Two really up-to-the-minute translations are 'Good News for Modern Man' which puts the New Testament into everyday English complete with pin-men illustrations, and the Living Bible which makes the whole Bible read like a novel. Use one of these side by side with your Authorised or RSV, and let one light up the other.

What do you read?

Make a start with the gospel of John, which will teach you so much about Jesus Himself, and what He offers to and expects of His followers. If you need help with knowing how much to read at a time, and explanation of the difficult parts, Scripture Union publish a booklet to read with St John's gospel called 'Invitation to Live' which does just that. When you have read St John, you may like to use the Scripture Union Bible reading scheme, which aims to take you through the Bible over a period of 5 years, alternating readings from the Old Testament with those from the New.

But whatever scheme you use, and whichever part of the Bible you are reading, start off by asking God to speak to you as you read. Then read the verses slowly and carefully, and ask yourself some questions (you may like to write the answers down in a notebook) such as:

1 Do I understand what this is all about? If the answer is 'no', try reading the same verses in another version.
2 What does this passage teach me about God, the Father, the Son and the Holy Spirit?
3 What does it teach me about life? Is there a warning, a good example, a promise or a command for me to obey?
4 Is there a verse, or part of a verse, which has something special to say to me that I can remember and think about during the day?

Mary likes to read her Bible in this way. She reads the verses that she has chosen for that day straight through, and then goes back to the beginning and looks at one or two verses at a time with the help of the questions. As God the Holy Spirit brings points to her notice she stops and prays about them before going any further. In this way, God speaks to her and then she answers. For instance, when she read in the gospel of Mark of Jesus getting up very early to pray, she realized that there was an example for her to follow. So she prayed straightaway for help to get up before the family were astir to talk to God – and then she set her alarm to go off earlier the next morning! Listen to God speaking to you, answer

Him and then take action. This is one of the ways that Christians grow up.

Prayer is talking to God

There is more to prayer, however, than talking to God about what you have just read in the Bible, important though this is. And this is where many people get stuck. There are libraries of books written on the subject of prayer, and we can go on learning more and more of what it means really to communicate with God throughout the whole of our lives. But these simple things are always true: prayer is talking to God anywhere, at any time and about anything.

Prayer is talking to God. If you have been brought up in a church where the prayers are read out of a book, or your only real contact with praying is the Lord's Prayer which you mumbled mechanically in school assembly, then the idea of just talking to God may seem very strange. But make a start at this point. God knows you through and through; He sees your every fault, every good point, every thought. He loves you just as you are. So there is no need to put on an act. God is the one person in the whole world with whom you can be completely open, so talk to Him – about everything. And if you still feel that you need some sort of a peg to hang your thoughts on, then try thinking of the book of the Bible, ACTS, like this.

A – Adoration – praising and worshipping God for what He is and all that He has done. Reading a psalm or the verse of a hymn can sometimes help us to put our thoughts into words.

C – Confession – thinking about God's holiness leads us on to realize our own shortcomings and so we confess them to God.

T – Thanksgiving – for forgiveness and every good gift that God showers on us so freely.

S – Supplication – praying for the needs of others and ourselves.

Whatever form of words you use, you can talk to God just where you are. You do not have to be in a church building to pray; and it is not essential to close your eyes or kneel down. There are times when you will do all of these things. But you can also pray while you are washing the dishes, polishing the floor or driving the car – and at these times it is probably best to keep your eyes open!

And you can talk to God at any time of the day or night – He is always listening. Most Christians like to talk over the coming day with God, as soon as they can after they are awake, but it is a pity to let it stop there. You can ask for help with a problem, admit that you have done wrong and ask for forgiveness, pray for the needs of friends and family just as the need arises. This is what the Apostle Paul meant when he said, 'Pray without ceasing'. We cannot spend all our time on our knees, but we can be in constant touch with headquarters. And no detail is too small for God to bother with; no problem too huge to bring to Him with complete confidence.

But perhaps you are saying that all this talk of Bible reading and praying is all very well, but however am I expected to find the time? If you feel like this don't worry – you are not alone. Finding time to be quiet and alone to pray and read the Bible is always difficult, and yet it is essential, if you are to grow as a Christian.

So when shall it be? As we have thought already, early in the day is ideal, before the pressure and rush really gets under way. Then you can bring all the details of the day to God and ask for help where you know that you will need it, and hear God speaking to you as you read the Bible. But perhaps you feel that it would bring the wrath of the rest of the household down around your ears if your alarm shrills out too early - well, God can waken you without an alarm if you ask Him to! Or if you are one of those folk who are not fully conscious until after breakfast, then pick up your Bible as soon as the family are dispatched for the day. Even toddlers at home can learn to be reasonably quiet while you 'talk to Jesus'. So don't tune your violin after the concert is over; fight for those few minutes early on in the day to get in touch with Jesus, and then you will find it so much easier to spend the rest of the day in harmony with Him.

3 *Sharing the good news*

Good news just asks to be shared! And when you come to realize what the good news of the Christian faith is all about, it's natural to want to rush off to family and friends and tell them what they are missing! You long for them to share your joy and peace. You want to discover God's purpose, not just for you as an individual but for the whole family unit.

It may be that your husband and older children have shared in your search for a purpose in life. If so, they will be delighted to hear about your new found faith and to explore it with you. But do not be too disappointed if the reaction of your family is very different. The Bible tells us that people who are not Christians are blind to the truth about God, until God Himself opens their eyes. Remember too that a sense of need is essential before we can accept what God has to offer, and the journey to the point of admitting that need is often long and slow.

Perhaps your nearest and dearest are of the opinion that 'a little bit of religion is fine for Mum if it keeps her happy' but don't want to know for themselves. Maybe they are downright sceptical about the very existence of God and would label themselves 'Humanist', 'Atheist', 'Agnostic' or simply 'Not Interested'. Whatever the situation that exists behind your front door, don't be discouraged. We are told in the Bible to be witnesses for Jesus. Now a witness is someone who has first-hand experience to share. And there are more ways of obeying that commandment than standing in the middle of the kitchen floor preaching a sermon. Let's think of some of them.

First of all, how do you announce the New Birth?

There's a time to speak

Christine became a Christian after three long years of searching, doubt and indecision. She had heard about what Jesus Christ had to offer, had been to church on and off, and was impressed by the 'extra something' that she sensed in the lives of some of the other young wives that she had met there. But although she longed to share their faith, she hung back for one very good reason – her clever scientist husband was openly scornful of anything to do with the Christian faith.

So on the night that she decided to accept what Jesus offered, whatever the cost, Christine went home with very mixed feelings. Should she tell her husband or not? Yes, after all their discussions, she felt that she must tell Stuart about the step that she had taken, and braced herself for the explosion that she expected to follow. It didn't come. Stuart heard her faltering explanation without interruption, and then lowered his newspaper for long enough to say mildly, 'Oh well, give it a try if you like, and we'll soon see if it really changes anything'. No more was said, but from then on, in his eyes, Christine's life was going either to prove or disprove the reality of the Christian formula.

And a time to keep silent

Mary thought that being a Christian meant going to church – and a very churchy person she was. She did all the right things, and went to lots of services, but that is where it began and ended. There was no inward change in her life, and her family were not at all impressed with her version of Christianity. Then one day she went to hear a missionary talk about his work in India, and heard instead how she could make a fresh start with Jesus Christ. Hardly daring to believe it, Mary took the first step of handing her life over to Jesus, and asked Him to do for her what the church services alone could not do – make her different. Of course she wanted to tell her husband that she had found the real thing at last, but she had preached at Don once too often in the past. So Mary felt that she must go home, say nothing, and live a new life, in this way proving to herself and her family that something had really happened.

For Mary actions came first. Christine had to prove the truth of what she said by what she did. And this is true for all Christians. Home circumstances and reactions vary so much, but however you try to explain your commitment to Jesus, it is your actions that will prove the reality and will make the most impression on those who know you best. So if actions speak more convincingly than words, how can you start to share Jesus with the family through what you do?

First of all, ask the Lord to show you where changes are needed in practical ways, and concentrate on one thing at a time.

Mary was married to a farmer who got up at a

very anti-social hour to see to the animals. Never once in their married life had Mary cooked his breakfast – in fact he cooked hers. So the first step in Mary's 'no speaking – all action' campaign was simple – she got up and cooked Don's breakfast. Not just once, but every day. And that was just the beginning of the revolution that Jesus brought about in her everyday life. Little by little He showed her where she was falling short in the ordinary practical things of life, and little by little enabled her to make changes. Since she had been a very 'don't-carish' sort of home-maker in the past, Don could not help but see the difference.

Perhaps you have always been a model housewife, so that you don't need to change in this particular way. But in every marriage there are points of friction where a change in your attitude would really show. Just one word of warning here. Make sure that the change you are making is one that brings pleasure to the other person, and not just to yourself. Let's see how this works out.

The garden was the gremlin that came between Sally and Clive. In Sally's eyes the garden was a man's job – her father had always done everything in her parental patch. In Clive's childhood the garden had been as much a part of his mother's domain as the house – and he did not expect to do more than mow the lawn occasionally. When Sally became a Christian she decided to try and share Jesus with her husband by making their home even more comfortable and attractive – a job that she loved. She went to flower arranging classes and took up patchwork – she enjoyed it all immensely and made lots of new friends.

She was rather hurt when this way of witnessing

to Clive cut very little ice. But as the flower arrangements made him sneeze and his favourite ancient sports shirt had been commandeered for the patchwork it was not altogether surprising. It took Sally a little while to see that she was on the wrong track. Then the horrid truth dawned. The change in her that the Lord wanted to see lay outside the house and in her private battle-ground, the garden. It was quite an inward struggle for a day or two, but when at last with a shrug and a smile Sally put away the patchwork and went out and bought a pair of gardening gloves, Clive did not need to be told that something real had happened in her life.

With Jenny it was not patchwork, it was baking. She loved cooking and cake-making was her speciality. So when she wanted to make up to her husband for some difference of opinion, or to show him what a good Christian wife she was, she would bake a cake. It was always a first class cake, but the only trouble was – Paul did not like cake very much. He would much rather that she had made love to him.

Don't let it shock you to think that Jesus can be shared in this most intimate part of marriage. The physical relationship can be the source of tremendous joy or considerable friction. And far from a wife leaving her husband, or moving into a separate bedroom when she becomes a Christain, the Bible says quite clearly in I Corinthians 7.13, 'If a Christian woman has a husband who isn't a Christian, and he wants her to stay with him, she must not leave him'. But more than that, verse 3 of the same chapter says, 'The man should give his wife all that is her right as a married woman, and the wife should do the same for her husband' (Living Bible).

So this means being the very best sort of wife in every sense of the word. Perhaps you need to ask His help in making a good relationship even better. Maybe your marriage has been a trifle 'mini' in this respect – you making the minimum response to his minimum requirements, and making excuses for the rest. If so, be glad that Jesus can help you change in this realm too, and a very powerful witness this can be.

Actions may speak louder than words but there will be a time and a place for words too. When comments are made about the changes in your life don't be afraid to explain why and give Jesus the credit. Resist the temptation to preach or argue about 'the Church' or 'Religion'. You may have to agree to disagree about theology but you can talk with confidence about what Jesus has done for you. If your actions bear you out, no one can disprove that!

So far we have thought about being witnesses for Jesus to your immediate family and friends. But what about those outside your immediate family circle? Should you rush off to offer your services to that understaffed Sunday School; the Old People's Friday Fellowship; or the faithful few who distribute the church magazine? It is very easy to feel that you are only doing something that counts for Jesus, if that something takes place outside your own home. And if the family are disinterested or unresponsive to your efforts to show them what it means to be a Christian, then it seems much more rewarding to concentrate your efforts elsewhere.

Think and pray carefully, however, before you

take on regular Christian activities that will take you out of your home a great deal. If God has given you a home and a family, then it is to that family that you have the first responsibility to take Jesus. If you are a new Christian you will have a lot to learn before you can teach other people. This does not mean that you have to be a theologian before you can be a witness for Jesus, but it is important to know what you believe and why. Of course Sunday School teachers and the like are needed, and it may well be that you will be asked to serve God in this way in due course. But in the meantime, do not despise the days of small things. The shopping done for the elderly neighbour, the toddler you can look after while his mother goes into town, being ready to do the extra run on the school ferry service for a mother with a sick baby – all these can be done as a service for the Lord, and can give opportunities to spread the Good News in deed as well as in word. Each day will bring its own opportunities – reach out and take the ones He gives with both hands.

So much for words and actions in 'Sharing the Good News'. There is another side of the coin which is even more important.

'Sometimes talk to those around you about God. Always talk to God about those around you.' This is the essential part of being a witness for Jesus that can never be overdone. Unless we are in touch with headquarters ourselves, we can work and talk until we are exhausted, and it will have no effect at all. But when we pray, God can work through us.

Perhaps you are saying, 'If this is so, why have I been praying for my husband to become a Christian for ages, and nothing seems to happen?' Well, there is more involved in prayer than just begging God to reveal Himself to those we love. What about your motives – why are you praying so earnestly for your husband, child or friend? Is it because you feel your life would be so much easier, your happiness more complete if your loved ones shared your faith? Be honest now! Or is it because you want them to know the joy of life with Jesus and to face death without fear? Of course these longings will prompt you to pray and it is right that they should. But what about God's part in all this? He is the One who has gone to such lengths to make it possible for people to come back to Him, and your first motive for praying should be for His own sake and glory. Then we should pray for the sake of the person concerned. You come into it last of all! When God brings you to see this, and enables you to pray with true unselfishness, you will begin to see those prayers having positive answers.

So pray for guidance in your actions. Pray for wisdom in what you say and what you do not. And pray for the work of the Holy Spirit, to open the eyes of your loved ones to their needs and His resources. Always remember that God is not depending on you to make anyone a Christian. You have your part to play, but you cannot do the Holy Spirit's work for Him. So, being a witness for Jesus is, as Campus Crusade for Christ puts it, 'Sharing Jesus, in the power of the Holy Spirit, and leaving the results to God'. And this you can do with absolute confidence.

4 *The children*

'I was so thrilled with Jesus that I just had to tell someone about Him, so I talked to Simon.' Barbara was talking about her early days as a Christian to her friends in their weekly Bible study group. 'He hadn't started school then and we were at home together all day. It was tremendous to see his faith flicker into life and grow.'

'Are you suggesting that a child of that age can have a personal faith – surely it's just that anything you say is right in their eyes just because you have said it?' Christine, the scientist's wife sounded dubious.

'Yes, I do believe that the Holy Spirit can help even a small child to have a personal faith – Simon certainly had one and still has. But I agree that it is a frightening amount of influence that "Mum" has on the under tens, and needs to be very carefully used. You know, there's the danger of them saying that they believe, just to please you, if they know that that's the answer you want. And that's hopeless. It's got to come from the child himself.'

'There's no danger of that with my two horrors,' said Jane plaintively. 'It's almost impossible to get them to church without a row. They know that their father rarely goes to church, and no ten or twelve year old wants to sit still for more than two minutes at a time anyway, so of course they don't want to come with me.'

'I think that lots of boys – and girls too for that matter – go through a "church hate" phase at that sort of age.' Elizabeth was the oldest member of the group and the mother of a teenage family. 'And it happens in homes where both parents are Christians, as well as those where they are not. My children were well into their teens before I became a Christian even, and it was no good thinking that I could frog-march them off to church. But when they noticed changes in me, then they were curious and started coming along sometimes to try and find out what was going on.'

'Yes, I think that's the key with older children,' Sally joined in the conversation rather shyly. 'I was getting into a terrible stew the other night because Clive was hours late getting home, and hadn't rung or anything. And Penny said to me, "Mummy, I thought Christians weren't supposed to worry". It brought me up with quite a jerk, especially as we've never really talked about me being a Christian before.'

'Well, I don't think I can have changed very much – or not so as my family would notice,' said Jane mournfully. 'And what do you *do* if they don't seem to want to know. I mean, it's bad enough having to worry about their school work, and who their friends are, and how much freedom to give them without this as well. And really it underlies all the rest doesn't it? How *do* you teach children about Christian things in this materialistic age, and get it across to them that it's real – the only reality, in fact, in spite of what they might hear from other people?'

Well, how do you? How do you start to share the

reality and excitement of living day by day with Jesus, with the children in *your* family who may vary in age from toddlers to teenagers?

If, like Barbara, you are at home all day with under fives, you will have plenty of opportunity to talk to them quite naturally about Jesus, through the questions they ask from morning to night. You know the sort of thing.

'Why are you reading that book, Mummy?'

'This is God's special book; it's called the Bible and tells us all about Him.'

'Who's God?' – a natural lead in to explaining God in terms of creation; something even a small child can begin to grasp.

'Why have you got your eyes shut, Mummy? Wake up!' Prod, prod!

'I'm talking to God, and asking Him to help me with all my jobs today. In a minute we'll talk to Him together.'

If you have to have your own Bible reading and prayer time after breakfast, or at some other time when the children are around, this can be a good time to give them a Bible story book to look at, and then a Bible story and prayer can follow your own prayer time. If time is short then perhaps after lunch might be a good time to tell or read a Bible story. The important thing is that Jesus should be seen to be an integral part of everyday life.

Of course, questions will not be reserved for times like these. Small children ask the most unexpected things at times, and take our replies very literally. When our second son was about a year old, I was sorting out some baby clothes. Our almost three year old son was helping and soon wanted to know what I was going to do with all these things. I explained that we would put some of the things away safely, in case we had another little baby to wear them, and give the others away to little babies who had nothing to wear.

'But are we going to have another baby?' he wanted to know. This was a bit of a poser as my husband and I were still praying this one over.

'Daddy and I will have to ask the Lord Jesus whether He wants us to have any more children,' I parried.

'Well, I want to ask Him now,' said David firmly. So, somewhat taken aback I prayed a short prayer asking that Jesus would show us whether He wanted us to have another baby or not. Our telephone age child opened his eyes and gazed at me expectantly.

'Did He say yes or no?'

So questions come and go, and get more complicated as the children grow older. It is a good principle to keep answers simple and to the point, without giving more information than is being asked for at that time. Some questions have to be answered many times before the answer is really grasped, but in an effort to be simple, never say something that you will have to unsay later.

There are of course many questions that have no simple complete answer, and it is never wrong to admit that you do not know. If the answer can be found, then look for it together; if it is one of life's imponderables, then say so, assuring them at the same time that God is all knowing and can safely be left to care for these things. This may sound trite, but it is true.

What happens if school teaches one thing and you another? In a sense this clash of views has to come sometime, and every child has to face it. It is often helpful if some other Christian adult can talk over these problems as well as yourself, so that they can see that other people believe these things as well as mother. In addition, there are many helpfully written books on such subjects as evolution, the evidence for the resurrection, and so on, and some of these are listed at the end of the book. Read and discuss them together, and then stand aside prayerfully and leave the Holy Spirit to do the job of conviction that only He can do.

So look on questions as an opportunity, not a threat, and do not be embarrassed if these questions come up when other adults are present. Sue's husband first came to realize that his idea of what the Christian faith was all about was quite different from hers simply by hearing her answer the children's questions. It was at this point that his own search for God began.

It is a very difficult calling to be a Christian mother in today's world when materialistic or even downright anti-Christian pressures bombard our children from every side. In what way should our Christian standards influence the way we run our homes? Can these standards be laid down for young lives that may not understand or agree with them? Well, all products operate best when used according to the maker's instructions, and this applies every bit as much to children. The Bible has much to say about family life, but it is sufficient for our purposes to look at three basic needs that are God-instilled in everyone, and this includes children. They are things that every Christian mother can try, with God's help, to provide.

A sense of identity

Everyone needs to be a person in his or her own right. God recognized this in His dealings with people in the Bible, and met with them as individuals, calling them by name. This sense of being an individual, a person who counts, is terribly important to all of us. So teach your children that they each have a special part in God's love, and that He knows them by name and has a plan for each individual life. And if you have more than one child, try to avoid lumping them all together. You know the sort of thing. 'The children', we say, or 'the boys'. Not 'Jill and Amanda' but 'the twins'.

When bedtime comes, try to spend a short time with each child, talking to him, hearing his news, and, if he is at an age when he is happy to do this, helping him to read his Bible and to pray. Scripture Union produce Bible story notes and aids for children from four years old and upwards, and it is at this time that queries and problems about the Christian faith can be brought into the open. Although it is very tempting to 'do' two children together, especially if they share a bedroom, and you are tired and longing for a bit of peace and quiet, resist it if you can. Apart from the fact that two is company and three is very much a crowd when it comes to sharing secrets, the problems of one child can easily confuse another, and a small 'first term at schooler' needs things explained in quite a different way from his 'just in the juniors' brother.

And when it comes to praying, pause for a moment and ask the Lord for a sense of His reality and nearness and then avoid the mechanical 'bless everyone in the world. Amen' approach. Even here the individual touch comes in. 'God bless Grandma' – but what particular blessing does she need? Not just 'God bless Daddy' but 'Help Daddy with that special job of work he has to do'.

The need to be accepted

'You're the odd one out!'
'No, I'm not!'
'Yes, you are.'

Now our children hate to be told that – do yours? We all need to be accepted by those around us, and so many of us, children included, spend anxious hours trying to appear what we are not, so as to keep 'in' with our particular crowd.

One of the most restful things about being a Christian is the knowledge that God accepts us as we are, not as we ought to be. Does this knowledge enable you to accept your children for what they are? Can you encourage them to develop their own God-given potential to the full? God intends that we should. We may have to face up to the fact that Mary will never be a ballet dancer, but will probably find her niche in life as a computer programmer; that Steve will never reach university, but has all the makings of an excellent mechanic. Can your children, especially the older ones, hold different views from you about politics, about their future plans, and, most difficult of all, about Christianity, without getting the feeling that you would love them much more if they thought as you do?

God's love is never conditional and we need to pray for this kind of love, again and again and again.

Children should be able to express their doubts and queries without any fear of being less acceptable to you. Above all avoid the situation where there is an unspoken division between those who are Christians and those who are not - Mummy's side and Daddy's side, or however the division falls, with the one group consciously or unconsciously looking down on the other. Always remember that any Christian who is trying to share his or her faith, is simply one beggar telling another beggar where to find bread.

Having told them, we must prayerfully stand aside and allow them to make their own choice about whether to go and find it. It is the hard way but the only way. A family that can acknowledge the importance of each individual, and can give everyone their right to be themselves, accepted and loved for what they are, will certainly have their share of lively discussion. They may lack the superficial peacefulness of those who insist on an outward conformity to one pattern. But it is an atmosphere in which God can work, because this is His way with people too.

Absolute freedom within clearly defined limits

Having said that children should be accepted as the individuals that they are, does not mean that they should be allowed to do exactly as they like. Family life would be unbearable if every member did his own thing with total disregard for the needs and convenience of others. Children need to be trained to be considerate, helpful, responsible and obedient. And in setting certain limits to acceptable behaviour, we are following the pattern of God's dealings with man, right from the beginning of time. In the very first chapters of the Bible we see how God gave man complete freedom and authority over his surroundings, except for one thing. And when this condition was broken, the inevitable consequences followed. You can read about it in Genesis 3.

So parents need to settle between themselves the boundaries of behaviour that are appropriate for the age and stage of their children, and make sure that the children understand what is expected of them, the reasons why and the penalty for disobedience. If only one parent is, as yet, a fully committed Christian, then you may not be able to arrange things in the way that you would consider ideal, but having decided on a workable arrangement (with much prayer beforehand) stick to it and back each other up at all times. Children need the security of united parents and although they may kick against the rules laid down for them, it is nevertheless a welcome safety barrier behind which to retreat when the pressures of the gang get too hot to handle.

And so we come to the final weapon – prayer. We can do our best, in our own strength, to guide our family life according to God's principles and perhaps produce a reasonably happy and well-balanced home. But if we are to lead our children to find their place in God's plan, knowing that they are accepted by Him, and experiencing the security and peace of living within the framework of His laws, the whole operation has to be bathed in prayer.

Firstly praying that God will so work in our own lives, that we can be, in His strength, the sort of mother He can use. And then bringing every day and every problem in the day to Him for His guidance and help. Things may not work out according to your plan. Life probably won't be cosy – the Holy Spirit has a habit of turning our preconceived notions upside down. But if we live life in this way, we can say with Paul 'We know that in everything God works for good with those who love Him' (Romans 8.28). Do we need any greater assurance for the well-being of our families than that?

5 *The day that is different*

'Sunday? It's the busiest day in the week! All the family want to do something different, and I seem to spend my day making sandwiches and getting meals at odd times – once I've got them out of bed that is!'

'Sunday? I would like to spend it just thinking about God – absolute quietness to worship and read . . . but of course, the family . . . '

'Sunday was a dreary day when I was a child. "Don't do this, don't do that" . . . I wouldn't want my children to hate it like I did, so it's very much like any other day for us.'

'Being a working wife, I have to spend the week-end catching up with the chores, but I do try to get to church once, most Sundays, and I think that is all that God expects.'

Four very different views of the first day of the week – as different as the personalities and circumstances of the women who expressed them. What sort of day is Sunday to you? Perhaps it was just the second day of the weekend before you became a committed Christian, but now you are wondering whether there should be any difference in this area of your life. Maybe you feel that 'keeping Sunday' went out with the Victorian age and you are glad that it did, with all its restrictions – and yet you have an uneasy feeling that it would be much easier if some time were to be automatically set aside for

God, in the rush and tear of everyday living.

Whatever our personal opinions may be, there is no doubt that the Bible teaches that one day in seven should be different. In fact, so important was this in God's scheme of things that it was included in the ten foundation laws for the Israelites' national life that we know as the Ten Commandments.

A day to remember

When Moses passed on God's laws to the Israelites for the first time he told them that the Sabbath (their equivalent of our Sunday) was to be set apart for God, so that they could worship Him, and remember how He had set them free from the slavery of Egypt.

They had a great deliverance to celebrate, but Christians have a far greater one, as they think each Sunday of the resurrection of Jesus and the way back to God that He has made for them. So Sunday is a day to remember, and for most of us this means going to church.

Is it necessary to go to church?

Going to church does not *make* you a Christian, but once you *are* a Christian you need the family of Christians who meet to worship in a local church, and that church needs you. The Bible speaks quite plainly about this. 'Let us not neglect our church meetings as some people do, but encourage and warn each other, especially now that the day of His coming back again is drawing near' Hebrews 10.24, 25 (Living Bible).

For a few Christian women, worshipping in church on Sunday (or, even more rarely, at all) is made impossible for a time because their husbands forbid it. But for most of us, whether our husbands accompany us, wave us off cheerfully as long as they are not involved, or merely tolerate our going, church going is possible if we are willing to make the effort.

Which church?

There is no such thing as a perfect church! How could there be when every church is made up of people, each with their own hopes and fears, strengths and weaknesses. But there is one particular group of Christians, working and worshipping together in your locality among whom God has a place for you. Your job is to find out which this is.

This is not always easy. Your natural inclinations may give you a preference for the hearty informality of a tiny mission hall, or the soaring beauty of a liturgical service in a great cathedral – or anything in between. You know that you need to belong somewhere where others know and love Jesus as a living Saviour and Lord. To help you grow as a Christian, you need to hear the Bible taught and explained as the inspired word of God that it is. Ideally your church should be local, so that you are worshipping and sharing Jesus with those among whom you live and work day by day. So there are many factors to consider before you find your ideal – and then be prepared for some surprises; God rarely works in 'ideals'!

So what are the guidelines which should shape your decision to join one particular church?

1 *Pray*

Talk to God about it, and ask Him to show you His choice, and to help you to accept it willingly.

2 *Look first at the familiar*

If you were already a fairly regular worshipper at one particular church before you became a committed Christian, stay where you are, unless or until God shows you that you should move.

Sally was in this position. Some of her Christian friends pressed her to leave the staid traditional church in which she had worshipped for several years. In many ways she would have liked to, but having prayed about it, she just could not feel that this was the right thing to do. Sally was well aware that she needed more help in understanding the Bible than she was getting from the Sunday services, so she asked a Christian friend to meet her for Bible study once a week. The group soon grew from two to a dozen, some of them from Sally's church. For many of these women, hearing the Bible explained in practical terms was something quite new and most exciting, and so God started to work in a new way in this church.

Jane's experience was different. She had worshipped at Sally's church for a long while, but when she became a Christian – through what she had heard at the Bible study group – God led her to a church of a different denomination for two or three years. There she learned much about the Bible and the Christian life, and grew up as a Christian in a very real way. But God did not leave her there. Having equipped her in this way, He showed her through circumstances that she must go back to her original church, and help Sally to share the reality of their faith with others in that particular congregation.

3 Summing up the strange

If you have no links with any church, talk to any Christian friends you may have, and visit their churches a few times until you get the inner sense that this is God's place for you. You've moved since you became a Christian? Then look first for a church which meets together during the week for Bible study and prayer. And above all be prepared to give as well as to receive – God can and will work miracles in a fellowship where there are even two or three who are prepared to pray and find out His will, and then do it.

Who goes and how often?

Ideally the whole family worships together at at least one of the Sunday services. Is this ideal completely removed from your reality? Don't despair. Keep the ideal in mind and work towards it, but be prepared to be adaptable, like Barbara.

'Church! church! church! That's all I seem to hear about these days!' Sam was letting his feelings be known in no uncertain terms! 'I like our Sundays as they are, and so did you until a few months ago. I'm not giving up my running on Sunday morning just so that you can go and waste your time in that church. If you want to go, you'll have to take the kids with you, and that's that!'

As you can see, Barbara had a problem. The church she attended provided a creche for tinies, but that was all, and the service was just not suited to the needs of restless under-elevens. Afternoon Sunday School and the evening service were out of the question – Sunday tea with his mother was something else Sam was not prepared to give up. The solution to the problem was found as Barbara prayed it over with a Christian friend. She introduced Barbara to a church where the Sunday morning service was a family service in which the odd whisper or dropped hymn book went unnoticed, and a Sunday School for the children during the sermon provided teaching that they could understand. And from then onwards church going for Barbara and the children was relatively friction free. Others have to make different concessions for the sake of family harmony.

Like Sam, Diana's husband is not very sympathetic about her church going, and would never go himself. At the moment Diana keeps the peace by getting up for the early morning service, so that his day is not interfered with, and her children go to a morning Sunday School. Janet does the extra Saturday preparation necessary to enable the whole family to drive ten miles to church – because this is the one church to which Tim will consent to go. As Mike insists on Sunday lunch being served on the dot of 12.30, Sue goes to church on Sunday evening. So be adaptable but you be there – if it is humanly possible.

Of course you will want to do everything in your power to encourage the rest of your family to be there with you. Younger children will probably be happy to come with you to a suitable service or Sunday School. Husbands and teenagers respond far better to a smiling casual invitation than a long face and nagging! Be open to the possibility that an invitation (by someone else!) to an organization like Crusaders or an after church squash and discussion may have far more appeal for your teenagers than the Sunday morning service. And remember above all that nothing is gained and much is lost if the matter of church going becomes a battleground. So if you have to go alone for a while, go cheerfully and ask God to make such a difference in your life and behaviour that the rest of the family will be drawn, in spite of themselves, to discover the reason why.

A day to rest

Few of us who are busy wives and mothers would argue about the need for a day of rest. And this too is part of God's plan for all His creatures. Moses was quite specific about it. Every one of the Israelites, from the master of the house down to the humblest employee, was to have one day in seven free from his regular work.

And yet while acknowledging the need, few of us take any practical steps to obey the command. 'A woman's work is never done', we quote glibly, and then wonder why, having ignored the Maker's instructions, we do not function or cope with life as well as we could.

Is it possible to make Sunday a 'day of rest' when you have a husband and family depending on you? Yes, it is possible, but it is not easy, and requires determination and discipline to achieve it. It is very easy to start off with a rush of enthusiasm, and for two or three weeks keep up to date with the chores, and do the extra preparation on Saturday, so that Sunday can be a rest day. Then comes a Saturday when you are extra busy, so you shelve just a few jobs 'until tomorrow' and the rot sets in.

So first of all, settle the principle in your heart. 'On Sundays I keep the routine chores down to a minimum because this is something that God has ordered for my good, and it is a command for me to obey.' Now obviously the things that constitute 'routine chores' will vary from household to household. A mother with a baby and young children will have more to do than one with older teenagers. And we must avoid copying the example of the religious leaders in Jesus' time (and others like them since) who made the do's and dont's for Sunday such a burden that the spirit behind it all was lost completely.

There is no need to feel that the family will suffer, or miss the special meals that are a feature of Sunday in many households. Vegetables can be done in a double batch on Saturday, a sweet prepared ahead, cakes made. A quick dust and tidy round on Saturday will cut out the need for any real housework, and if you see a cobweb on Sunday, ignore it with a clear conscience – it's your day off!

The family may find this new policy a little strange at first, but even if they cannot appreciate the spiritual reasons behind it most folk would agree that mother has a right to one day off a week. Especially so when they reap the benefit of having someone who is much more able to cope with the stress and strains of the other six days, at the centre of the family circle.

A day to rejoice

God intends us to be happy and enjoy this day which is His gift for our good, and yet this element of rejoicing often seems to be missing as we rest and remember God on His day. How can we make this day enjoyably different for all the family?

In this, as in everything else domestic, mother's attitude is all important. If our hearts are peaceful, because we are not worrying about weekday problems, and full of gladness, because Jesus is alive, then this will affect the whole atmosphere of the home. The ways we occupy the hours of Sunday that are not spent in worship will vary considerably from family to family. In those homes where the majority are committed Christians, activities will be quite different from homes where only one person loves the Lord Jesus. But whatever our circumstances, we can follow the example of Jesus as He worshipped, spent time with His disciples and was always ready to help those in need.

Enjoyment of God's good gifts often starts at a very practical level, so how about letting various members of the family choose their favourite food for one or other of the meals. Fresh brewed coffee for breakfast, squash instead of water for lunch time drinks, and sweets that are too expensive to be bought out of the children's sweet allowance, are some of the things which make Sunday special in our household. And it need not mean more work. Your family might prefer a picnic in the garden to a full blown roast on a summer Sunday; soup and sandwiches in the car are more fun than a dainty afternoon tea after a wintry afternoon in the country.

A day to communicate

'We just don't have time to talk these days; there's always one member of the family dashing off somewhere; we're all too busy.' If your house is more like Paddington station than a peaceful oasis from Monday to Saturday, then use Sunday to get to know each other a little better. It is no use complaining that your teenagers use the house like a hotel and never confide in you if you have been too busy to forge the links of communication when they were younger.

In our house, Sunday is Family day. Our children are not allowed to disappear off to play with their friends from dawn till dusk, but to compensate, each member of the family takes it in turns to choose what we do on Sunday afternoon (we have a morning Sunday School) and the rest are bound to abide by the chooser's choice, without grumbling. In this way we may spend one Sunday feeding the ducks down at the river, another stalking each other through the woods, a third entertaining another family to tea – but whatever is done, everyone joins in.

A day to share

'I want to give and give until it hurts,' sighed Kate. 'I want to share our home on Sunday with people who can't pay us back – old people, students, tramps even – but of course Jim doesn't see much further than his own family circle, so it's tea with relations most weeks.'

Here is another situation which can cause tension in many families. One member wants to use Sunday to share with everyone the good things that God has given; another feels family and close friends come first and others are a very poor second. What can you do if this is your problem?

Again the solution seems to be flexibility. It may be possible, sometimes, to invite the lonely and the needy to share your home on Sundays – but be equally willing to welcome those of the family who, though they may seem to have everything, are just as much in need of Jesus. However unsympathetic they may seem, you may be the only Christian they know – the only one who can demonstrate His love in action.

And if you cannot invite folk to your home, perhaps you can be like Sylvia who spends the hour that the children are at Sunday School and her husband is reading the papers, with the widow up the road. Or perhaps you can give Mrs A a lift to church when you go, or write a letter to Mrs B in hospital. There are so many ways of sharing God's goodness with others, so let this be a part of our Sunday too, doing what we can with a willing heart and above all, cheerfully, remembering that 'Cheerful givers are the ones God prizes' (2 Corinthians 9.7, Living Bible).

6 *You're not the girl I married!*

'The girl that I marry will have to be as soft and as pink as a nursery!' Well, that's one man's vision of his future wife; not quite in the modern idiom of long haired dolly girls perhaps. Nevertheless, it is very true that each one of us brings to marriage a mental picture of the husband or wife that is our 'ideal'. The way this picture takes shape depends on many factors. A girl is influenced more than she realizes by what her father was like, and whether or not she had a good relationship with him. The books she read and the television and films she saw in her pre-marriage years, all combine to give her a mental picture of the kind of man who will fulfil her particular needs and complement her character. And the same situation applies with a man.

While we may realize at the outset that our real life partner has a few of the 'ideal' characteristics missing from his make-up, we think, blithely, that within the framework of marriage we can make the one or two alterations necessary. What we often do not realize is that our partner may have the same plans for us, and it is at this point that trouble can start.

No doubt you have a pretty clear idea of what you want from your husband and marriage. And if you have been married for any length of time those ideas have had to be modified somewhat. But have you ever paused to consider, or even tried to find out, what your husband wants from his marriage? Is he basically unsure of himself, needing someone who can support, encourage and mother him? Perhaps he's a 'go-getter' who expects his wife to keep pace with him in his climb to the top, taking all the home responsibilities off his shoulders, so that he can give his mind to outside matters. Does he want a model housekeeper, feeling that home is only home if you are there all day and there are home-made cakes for tea – or will he cheerfully exist on convenience foods so that you can both go out to work?

Of course, over the years, every couple changes to a greater or lesser degree, being moulded by circumstance and the pressures exerted by their 'other half'. But when you become a committed Christian a new factor comes into the marriage which inevitably brings with it its own pressures and possibilities.

Some women mistakenly believe that when they become a Christian they have to abandon all their old friends and interests, neglect their appearance, and spend their time saying 'no' to things. Now of course there will have to be changes in your life, but make sure that they are those prompted by Jesus and not by your own ideas of what Christians should or should not do. Otherwise you may have to listen to your husband say, with absolute truth, 'You're not the girl I married and you're dull! dull! dull!'

If you put yourself in this position you are being unfair to your husband and to God. It is God's plan that His children should be better marriage partners not worse ones, and this we will be if we follow God's plan for the marriage relationship, and then make a real effort to understand our partner and his needs.

God's first requirement of us as Christian wives is *submission to our husband's authority*.

The very word sticks in your throat, doesn't it, in these days of 'Woman's Lib'? And yet the most ardent feminist has to admit that any team can have only one leader, and God has ordained that the leader in the marriage team is to be the husband. 'But surely,' you might argue, 'this only applies when the husband is a Christian'. That is not what the Bible says.

'You wives must submit yourselves to your husbands, so that if some of them do not believe God's word, they will be won over to believe by your conduct. It will not be necessary for you to say a word' (1 Peter 3.1, 2, TEV).

You may feel that you could never bring yourself to be genuinely submissive – in fact you bristle at the mere thought of it – and this is true for many of us. But if you are really willing to obey God's command, and tell Him so, He will take care of the emotions involved, and enable you to be, in His strength, what you could never be on your own.

How far does this submission take us? All the way, except on the rare occasion when submission to her husband would lead a wife to do something illegal or immoral.

'Wives, submit yourselves to your husband, as to the Lord' says Ephesians 5.22 (TEV).

This is the key. If you can fall in with your husband's wishes without, at the same time, disobeying any of God's commands, then you must do so. Occasionally the line dividing the one from the other is a very fine one. If this happens, pray about the problem very carefully before you act, and if there is an ultimate clash of loyalties remember that obedience to God comes first.

Submission to her husband does not make a Christian wife an inferior being and a doormat. She is still free to state her case, very lovingly, if she feels that her husband is leading the team in the wrong direction. But (and this is the hard part) if he is adamant, she must refrain from nagging and leave the final decision to him, trusting God to take care of the results. It may be better to pray than to speak on some occasions. God can overrule circumstances and influence decisions without our having to say a word – but remember that true submission is an attitude of heart and mind. It is all too possible to be outwardly submissive, with tight lips and a pained expression, and inwardly seething. This is not submission, and we cannot expect God to bless it. Perhaps this aspect of the marriage relationship can be summed up in St Augustine's words:

'Woman was taken out of man, not from his head, to be above him, nor from his feet to be trampled under foot, but from his side to help him, from under his arm to be protected by him and from near his heart to be loved by him.'

Two individuals – and yet one

God has planned that a wife should follow her husband's lead, but it does not mean that she should be her husband's shadow.

'I'm just somebody's wife, and someone else's mother.' Have you ever said that, feeling that your own personality counts for nothing? Well, you certainly count with God, and when you realize this and the fact that part of His overall plan in history can be fulfilled by you alone, then, perhaps for the first time, you discover a sense of personal identity. Life takes on a new dimension as you see God begin to work out His plan for your life.

Now while this is all to the good, beware of becoming so bound up with your new Christian friends and activities that your home and family take second place. Imagine how you would feel if your husband suddenly became absorbed in a purely masculine hobby with which you were neither able nor willing to be involved. Suddenly he wants to be out of the house several evenings a week; he has a new circle of friends with whom you just do not feel at home – you cannot even understand what they are talking about most of the time. Your whole family life has to change to accommodate this new hobby and gradually you feel more and more shut out. Of course, that does not apply to your Christianity . . . or does it? Yes, God intends that you should be an individual, but in marriage He also intends that the two should be one, and although your first allegiance is to Him, on the human level, your husband has the first call on your loyalty and love.

So let's 'accentuate the positive and eliminate the negative' as the song has it. Work at your marriage, being prepared, if you do not know already, to find out what your husband longs for in a wife, and trying to meet those needs. He does not talk about that sort of thing? Stray comments can give clues; those light hearted quizzes in women's magazines can be very revealing! And above all, the offer of God's wisdom applies in this, as in any other situation.

Welcome opportunities to meet people. Don't look on the social side of your life together, or of your husband's job, as something to be avoided wherever possible. There may be certain times when it is right to refuse an invitation, but remember that Jesus never cut Himself off from those who needed Him most. So, rather than running away, ask Him to keep you on these occasions and you will find opportunities in the most unlikely situations.

Barbara would have been glad to avoid the dinner dance given by Sam's firm, but there seemed to be no way of getting out of it. When she went to the powder room after dinner she knew why God had not given her an excuse to stay at home. A slight acquaintance was huddled in a corner sobbing bitterly. Within a few moments the whole story of a broken marriage came tumbling out.

'Help me, Barbara; give me something to cling on to . . .' And so, when she least expected it, Barbara was able to be the first link in the chain that eventually drew that woman to God.

What about the activities that used to fill your life that no longer appeal? Of course you will want to cut out those things that do not honour Jesus Christ, but if this means there are fewer things that you can do together, look for other interests that you can share with your husband. If lack of baby-sitters keeps you at home, then join a baby-sitting group or start one. Once you have got into the habit of going out together again, whether it is to friends, an evening class or local society, it will be more likely that he will be happy to accompany you to the church harvest supper, or a Christian friend's coffee evening.

Above all, don't be dull. Ask Jesus to fill your life with His joy so that you are a living example of one who is living the 'Life in all its fulness' that He came to give.

7 *A new kind of loving*

What does 'love' mean to you? It may be one thing at this moment, and something quite different tomorrow, because it is a word that we use very frequently to express a whole range of emotions. We speak of men murdering for love of money and dying for love of country and friends. We may claim to love our favourite food, an agreeable job and the area in which we live – but it is a very different emotion from that which we feel towards husband and family. And none of these feelings correspond exactly to that attitude of complete self-giving referred to by Jesus, when He commanded His disciples to 'love one another as I have loved you'.

As we all know, love should be the hallmark of the Christian; not as some bubbling super-happy emotional state, but as a practical standard to govern the whole of one's thinking and way of life.

1 Corinthians 13.4–8 spells out in very down to earth language exactly what the outworking of Christian love entails.

'Love is patient and kind; love is not jealous or boastful; it is not arrogant or rude. Love does not insist on its own way; it is not irritable or resentful; it does not rejoice in wrong but rejoices in the right. Love bears all things, believes all things, hopes all things, endures all things. Love never ends.'

If you are thinking that this is asking the impossible you are quite right – humanly speaking! For this is God's own love which He pours out, so that it might fill us and overflow as we truly love other people. But this does not happen without any action on our part. The apostle Paul tells us to 'make love your aim' (1 Corinthians 14.1). We can choose whether or not we will allow this love to flow; whether we are prepared to put aside our own rights and self-interest. God never forces anything upon us; not even love.

How does this work out in practice? Imagine a pipe – the sort that carries water from point A to point B. If it is to work efficiently it is essential that it should be whole. If there are cracks or gaps in the walls of the pipe its contents will soon seep out and the pipe will be empty. And so the Christian who wants to be a channel of God's love to a thirsty world must be whole-hearted about it. Too many of us want to play at being Christians – happy to accept the benefits it brings so long as it does not cost us anything. And a Christian like that is like a leaking pipe, giving out the merest trickle where there should be a flowing stream.

A water pipe must also be clean. Dirt and leaves that get into the pipe soon clog it up, and the flow is slowed down, and perhaps almost stopped. What hampers the flow of God's love in your life? Yourself? Self-interest, self-love – the attitudes that run quite contrary to the self-sacrificing love that St Paul describes? Perhaps it is disobedience, rebellion against some aspect of God's dealings with you, or unbelief, that is silting up the channel of your life. God knows and He will show you and deal with it if you really want Him to.

The most important thing of all for our water pipe is that it should be connected to the source of supply. And for Christians this means allowing the Holy Spirit to work in our lives. The Bible tells us that love is the first fruit, or result, of the Holy Spirit's activity in our lives – but again *we* have to *allow* Him to produce it. Every Christian has the Holy Spirit in his or her life, but the Holy Spirit does not 'have' every Christian. So many of us let the Holy Spirit have control of one small part of our life – but keep the rest of it very firmly in our own hands . . . just in case! This is not how God intends that we should live. The Bible tells us to be filled with the Spirit, so don't keep Him shut up in the kitchen of your life, but ask Jesus to give you His Spirit in all His fulness, so that His presence and power fills the whole house – from loft to sun-room! Don't be afraid of where this may lead you – it is an occupation of love to produce love, even in the most unlovely. And it is only as the Holy Spirit works that we can begin to put His love into practice with the one who needs and expects it most – your husband and mine.

Marriage has a greater potential for happiness or utter misery than any other human relationship. Of course no one gets married intending to be unhappy, and yet most of us know at least one couple who started so confidently together, and within a few years they are further apart in spirit than complete strangers. And yet if God created the marriage relationship, then surely He is capable of making it work. As the marriage service puts it, God planned that marriage should be 'for the mutual society, help and comfort' of the two people involved. Companionship, helping and comforting – how much of that goes on in your home? Or is there an atmosphere of armed neutrality, with two people both jealously guarding their rights? Whether your marriage is reasonably happy or downright miserable, God's love can transform this or any other relationship, if even one of the people involved will allow it to flow.

Love in Action

'There is always one who kisses and one who holds the cheek' – which one are you? Is your love patient and kind – with all that that involves? Are you as patient with his shortcomings as you expect him to be with yours? What about those little habits that seemed so endearing at first, and yet become more and more irritating as the years slip by? Is the Holy Spirit in charge of your tongue; do you try to comfort and build him up by what you say; or are you guilty, like so many of us, of the kind of verbal sniping which is more hurtful than any blow?

'Is it kind, is it true, is it necessary?' If we measured all our comments by that standard, far less would be said in many homes.

Now that you are a Christian there are, inevitably, some problems in your life that your husband finds it difficult to appreciate. Accept that fact, but *never* build the beginning of a barrier between you by telling him that only 'so and so' (another Christian) can possibly understand what is bothering you. If he is concerned because you are out of sorts, admit that you are feeling down (there is no need to go into details) and draw strength and comfort from the love that prompted that concern. And remember that God Himself is the One completely unbiased and fully sympathetic listener, who is always available, even if all that you have to say is that you don't feel like praying! He may provide you with a wise and trustworthy Christian friend, who can help and advise you with a problem, and this can be an enormous help. But do be sure that in sharing a confidence you refrain from those gossipy character shredding sessions that are beloved by so many women. 'Items for prayer' can so easily become 'characters to tear' – beware!

'Love is not jealous' – you know that and so do I! And yet this painful and damaging feeling can creep up on us almost unnoticed, causing many angry words and unhappy hours. It needs to be recognized for what it is – and dealt with. Can you be genuinely pleased when others succeed in a hobby or job – or do you feel let down and frustrated because your life seems dull by comparison? What about your husband's relationship with the children? How do you feel when he sets off with your son to a football match, men together, while you are left at home with the baby? Is it jealousy that makes you slam the kitchen door and shout at the cat? Or perhaps it's your daughter who shows the sunny side of her character to her father so that you seem to be the only one who ever corrects her. Jealousy is fear; fear of being less loved, less wanted, less successful – and perfect love, God's love, casts out fear (1 John 4.18). It is the perfect antidote for any and every jealous fear and uncertainty – apply it daily as required!

Days of small things

'It's not so hard to be loving over the big problems. It's the little things that are so irritating – like water dripping and wearing away the rock. It's not that Peter is anti-Christian exactly, but there are so many little details that we look at differently these days.' Jane was still rather a new Christian and she was finding the going hard.

'Take television for instance. I don't mind watching it when there is something good on, but I hate coming in from church on Sunday evening to find it blaring away – it's like coming into another world. And the way Peter moans if I want to give some extra money to any Christian appeals – and yet he spends more than I ever give on records each month; it's not fair! Then there's reading in bed. You wouldn't think that that would be a problem, would you, but I like to read my Bible last thing at night and it seems all wrong, me lying there reading my Bible while Peter is lying the other side of the bed reading his "blood and thunders" – I'd burn the lot if I was given half the chance.'

'Why is it all wrong?' Elizabeth was older in years and in the faith, and much wiser. 'Peter is only behaving as it is natural for him to behave. The way you behaved until not so long ago. It is you who are wrong, Jane, to expect him to behave like a Christian when he is not. It is quite natural that he should want to spend his money in the way that pleases him – there's no need for you to feel guilty if you are not able to give as much to Christian work as you would like to. God knows your motives and how much you are keeping back for yourself, and that's what counts with Him. So don't nag at Peter – about his taste in television programmes, books or anything else. If you do, you are suggesting that you will love him only if he conforms to your standards. And without Jesus in his life he's got neither the motive nor the power to do it.'

'I suppose you're right,' admitted Jane reluctantly, 'but what can I do about this bed-time business? It matters a lot to me. I want the Bible to be the last thing I read, so that it is filling my mind as I go to sleep, and I know Peter doesn't like it much. Not that he *says* anything, but there's . . . well, you know . . . an atmosphere.'

'Put yourself in his position,' Elizabeth suggested, 'and it's not hard to see why. Peter probably thinks it's all being done to impress him, and that puts his back up immediately. I mean, how would you feel if he lay reading "The Thoughts of Chairman Mao" and telling you that the novel that you were reading was an insult to the liberated mind of the common people! But one way round this problem would be to learn passages from the Bible by heart. This is a very good thing to do anyway, and you could be thinking these verses over last thing at night without upsetting anyone.

'As for the television problem – stamps solved that for us. Not that I realized that this would happen when I started to take an interest in John's stamp collection – I just wanted to share his interests more. Then somehow Sunday evening after church has become the time we get the stamps out and the television goes on less and less frequently. Sometimes John does want to watch it, and then I ask God to keep the peace and joy of the service singing in my heart, and drown those niggles of resentment with His love – and He does.'

The discipline of love

'If you love someone, you will be loyal to him no matter what the cost. You will always believe in him, always expect the best of him and always stand your ground in defending him' (1 Corinthians 13.7, Living Bible).

Is this another way of saying that love should ignore the faults in the beloved? 'Love is blind', we say, but although this may be so in human love, it is never true of God's love. God loves us while knowing all about our failures, but in His love, He orders our circumstances so that we are disciplined and trained and the failures and shortcomings which spoil our lives are gradually eradicated. And God's all-accepting love is to be our standard.

No two people can live together within the intimacy of marriage, without each one becoming all too aware of the other's faults. The trouble is that we are also all too ready to try and put each other right. And although it may be right on some occasions to point out a fault or a mistake, think very carefully about your motives before you rush in. Read Galatians 6.1 (TEV):

'My brothers, if someone is caught in any kind of wrongdoing, those of you who are spiritual should set him right; but you must do it in a gentle way. And keep an eye on yourself, so that you will not be tempted.'

'You who are spiritual' – does this describe you or would 'you who are glad to be in the right this time' be more appropriate? Are you gentle and humble? Have you been at fault in any way? Are you cherishing illusions about your own resistance to temptation? Is it necessary to *say* anything, or would it be better to pray, and leave the Holy Spirit to work?

Having thought and prayed through all these points, hand the whole matter over to Jesus. If it is His will for you to say anything to your husband, then He will make the opportunity for you to speak gently and with His love. If that opening does not come – keep quiet. God has other plans, and He will accomplish them in His own way, however impossible this may seem to you.

Love never ends

This kind of loving is not just to last for a day or a week or a month, but for ever. Do you feel that you could never keep it up on your own? You are quite right; you could not and neither could I. Jesus said it in John 15.5: 'Apart from me you can do nothing'. But the glorious thing is that we do not have to do it on our own. What we do have to do is to ask for His help day by day to keep the channel of our life whole, clean and connected to the mainspring of His love. Given our obedience in this, the Holy Spirit can produce this fruit of love which will shine like a beacon in your small corner of God's world, and which nothing and nobody can put out.

8 *'I'm a failure'*

So it's been one of those days! You woke up late feeling overwhelmed by the prospect of all you had to do, and from the moment you got out of bed everything seemed to go wrong. The children have been unmanageable, you've had a row with your husband and by bed-time you have come to the conclusion that there is nothing in this Christianity business after all. The future stretches ahead as a series of grey monotonous days ending in nothing and you don't even want to pray.

Have you had days or even weeks like that? There are few of us who have not. Perhaps life has not been particularly difficult, and yet the Bible seems as dry as dust and your prayers get no higher than the ceiling. Doubts about your faith come creeping into your mind, and before long you wonder if you can possibly be a Christian at all if you feel like this. What is the remedy for times like these, and how should we apply it?

First of all it is important to recognize the cause. One of the most basic causes of feminine moods is the monthly ebb and flow of the body's hormones. Much has been written on this subject, and there is no need to go into detail here, other than to say that the cause of pre-menstrual tension is not spiritual but physical, and the right steps to take, if it is very severe, are those in the direction of your doctor's surgery! So when you wake up feeling blue, check the calendar. You can't blame it on your hormones? Then how about other physical causes? Would a few early nights give you a different view of life, or a little less dashing around during the day?

If none of these simple, but often overlooked, causes apply to your 'off-day', then it is time to dig a little deeper. Are you trying to live the Christian life in your own strength, struggling to break with old habits and change yourself to be a carbon copy of the Christian that you most admire? Then stop trying! It is a demoralizing struggle and what is more it is a waste of time, because it is impossible. The only person that God wants you to be like is the Lord Jesus, and this is a gradual process, as we stop struggling to improve ourselves, and let the Holy Spirit mould us to His pattern. Every time we obey His prompting, every time we allow the patient love of Jesus to have the upper hand instead of the irritable love of self, we take one step forward. And even the difficult times of doubt and spiritual dryness can serve to drive our roots down deeper into the love of God if we recognize them as disciplines to help, instead of demons to destroy.

But perhaps the underlying cause of your problem is something more specific. Are you worrying about something, facing a problem with which you feel unable to cope? Paul has something to say about that:

'Have no anxiety about anything, but in everything by prayer and supplication with thanksgiving let your requests be made known to God. And the peace of God, which passes all understanding, will keep your hearts and minds in Christ Jesus' (Philippians 4.6).

So worry is disobedience, and as such sin. Take your problem to Jesus, ask for His wisdom and in faith thank Him for His help. Then take one positive step towards the solution. Treat it like a tree to be cut down. When foresters are felling trees, they do not go straight to the main trunk and hack away with a saw or axe. Instead they trim off the small branches first, and then the larger ones. It is only when these have been dealt with that they tackle the main trunk. And so it is with a problem that defeats you. Ask Jesus to show you what small part can be dealt with straight away. Lop that off and the whole thing seems a lot more manageable.

Maybe you are saying, 'It would be simple if I knew why I felt like this, and then I could deal with it, but I don't'. If this is the way you are feeling, ask the Holy Spirit to show you if there is something in your life that is festering away under the surface.

Do you look at other women and say to yourself, 'Of course I could be a radiant Christian like her if only . . . ! If only I was as placid as she is, or found it as easy to talk to people. If only my children were still young enough to do as I say – or old enough to be off my hands. If only Jim was like Clive, we would all be in church every Sunday – and if I had plenty of spare time like Sally I'd be a Sunday School teacher too.' If only, if only, if only . . . don't waste your time in wishful thinking. God has given you your temperament, time and talents. He has plans for your husband, your family and your particular opportunities for serving Him – accept them gladly as His gift. And give Him in return what He longs for most – yourself. Then all these other things will click into place, and you will learn the lessons that will enable you to be His person in your unique situation.

These then are some of the causes of spiritual despondency which attack us all from time to time. Sometimes we have to look outside ourselves and recognize that these difficult periods are a direct attack of the devil, aimed at discouraging us and making us less useful in God's service. This often happens after a time when we have been on the crest of the wave spiritually, and the Bible has the short answer to that situation. James 4.7, 'Resist the devil and he will flee from you'.

So while it is necessary, at times, to take a spiritual inventory, don't brood, but keep your eyes firmly fixed on Jesus. If you have Him you have all you need – claim it, and enjoy your inheritance. Too many Christians are like the Texas rancher who used to ride over his ranch, worrying about how he was to pay his bills. Little did he know that deep down under the surface of his land was an enormous oil field, which, once drilled, would make him a millionaire several times over. He owned the land and the oilfield and yet he was so poor that he was living on government assistance.

'My God will supply every need of yours' (Philippians 4.19) – do you believe it? Do you keep short accounts with God, asking for and accepting His forgiveness immediately the Holy Spirit makes you conscious of some sin in your life? Or do you labour along feeling guilty and out of touch with God because you have done the same thing today as you did yesterday, and you really can't expect Him to forgive you again. You might not expect it but you can accept it – 'There is therefore now *no condemnation* for those who are in Christ Jesus' (Romans 8.1) – and the voice that says that there is comes straight from the devil.

How about material needs? Do you believe that God will supply those? Notice that the word is *need* not *want*. You are unlikely to find a mink coat in a parcel on the doorstep, but if for instance, like Carol, you need money for fares to enable you to do some specific piece of Christian service you can trust Him to provide it. She did and was not disappointed. God's provision in material things is not limited to the George Müllers, Hudson Taylors and Brother Andrews of this world.

'To us a son is given; and the government will be upon his shoulder, and his name will be called Wonderful Counsellor, Mighty God, Everlasting Father, Prince of Peace' (Isaiah 9.6).

Is the government of your life on His shoulder? Then *you* can know Him in all these ways. Do you need wisdom? He is the wonderful counsellor who will guide and help you so patiently, no matter how slow you are to learn.

Are there problems in your life to which none of your friends or professional advisers can offer a solution? You have the ear of a Mighty God, with whom *all* things are possible.

Do you ever get tired of being 'Mum' – the one to whom everyone comes, expecting you to be strong, confident and always available? For those times you can turn to the Everlasting Father. Perhaps your human parents are no longer available to ease some of the strains of life – lean back on the everlasting arms; they will never let you down.

And last of all, in a world full of tension and hatred, we have Jesus as Prince of Peace. Say these words over to yourself . . . if you have Him, you are living in the constant company of the Prince of Peace. Do you let His peace rule in your heart? Claim this on 'one of those days' and although your circumstances may not change, at the centre of the storm there will be peace.

So don't condemn yourself for your failures. Bring them to Jesus and claim His resources, remembering that you are, as E. Stanley Jones puts it, 'neither worm nor wonder, but a bundle of possibilities in Jesus Christ'.

9 *'At home where it's hardest'*

It is harder to be a Christian at home, than almost anywhere else at all. Most of us find it easy to put on our best selves for the benefit of the outside world, but at home where there is no one to see us but those who think nothing of showing *us* their less pleasant sides, it is a different matter.

The Bible holds up a very high standard for wives and homemakers. If you have ever read the verses describing the 'Virtuous Woman' in Proverbs 31.10–31 you may have dismissed them as being written for another age. I mean, all this talk of 'rising while it is yet night' and providing 'food for her household and tasks for her maidens' – who has maidens to be set to work these days anyway? There is only one maiden in our household and that is me! Of course, it could not mean, in today's context, that she gets up in good time, gets the washing machine going and has an appetizing breakfast on the table for the family before they dash off to work and school . . . or could it?

Have a closer look at the Virtuous Woman, perhaps in a modern translation, and you will find that she is quite an up-to-date female. She is a business woman, a 'do-it-yourselfer', helps those less fortunate than herself and is the inspiration and architect of her husband's success. And if all that makes you want to creep away into the nearest corner and hide, take heart. Creating a home is a gradual process, and a homemaker grows along with it. After all, your first married home is probably very different from the one you live in today. And you may well have changed from a 'Can't-boil-an-egg Barbara' to a 'Soufflés-are-simple Susie'.

But the most important thing about a home in which Jesus has a part is not the furnishings, or your accomplishments as a cook, but the atmosphere. What do you contribute to the atmosphere of your home? Dr Norman Harrison compares the family circle to a wheel. Father is the rim coming as a protective cushion between the family and the world, and mother is the hub – everything in the home revolves round her. If the hub is off-centre the whole wheel is thrown out of balance. And we can see that this works out. When you wake up in the morning, full of eager anticipation for the day ahead, the morning starts well for all the rest of the family. And the reverse is equally true.

So does this mean that the atmosphere in your home is going to swing from happy to moody, from cheerfulness to silence, in direct relationship to the way you feel? It can do, when we lose touch with Jesus Christ. But in Him there is stability. James 1.17 says, 'With Him there is no variation or shadow due to change'. Hebrews 13.8 says, 'Jesus Christ is the same yesterday and today and for ever'. So if His life is flowing through you, you too can know the inner peace and stability that is not disturbed by the winds of circumstance that may ruffle the surface of your life. Of course this does not mean that the atmosphere of your home will be calm and peaceful at the precise moment when your husband has lost his car keys, your sons are quarrelling ferociously over the possession of a football coin, and the toddler has tipped the remains of her cereal onto the carpet for the cat! But it does mean that your whole day will not be ruined as you consciously put aside your irritation, and allow His peace and joy to have the upper hand.

1 Peter 3.3–4 (Living Bible) says, 'Don't be concerned about the outward beauty that depends on jewelry, or beautiful clothes, or hair arrangement. Be beautiful inside, in your hearts, with the lasting charm of a gentle and quiet spirit, which is so precious to God.' Have you ever thought that this verse might apply to you? Oh yes! you have heard that Christian women should be more concerned with what goes on in their personalities than what they put on their faces! But 'a gentle and quiet spirit', or, as another version puts it 'a calm and gentle spirit' . . . it came as a shock to me that this was a direct command and not just an optional extra for those who happened to be temperamentally suited to it!

So, if it is a command to be obeyed, how do we set about it? As with everything in the Christian life, there are two sides to our obedience. Firstly the command itself, and then the way that it works out in our everyday life.

What does having 'a gentle and quiet spirit' involve? We have already thought of the way in which we can allow the love, peace and serenity of Jesus to flow through us. But to be calm and gentle do we have to be wishy-washy and spineless? Not at all. There are times, especially with children, when they need to know that they have gone about as far as they can go, and know it in no uncertain terms. Does it mean that we should 'opt out' and just let the world pass us by, ignoring the problems? No, it does not.

Let's look at the question from a different angle. What is it in your life that stops you feeling calm, quiet and gentle? A fever? No, I don't mean the sort of fever that sends the mercury rocketing up inside the thermometer, but the ones that are equally damaging to our spiritual health and well-being. We speak of a fever of anxiety – are you a worrier? Or what about the fevers of resentment and rebellion – 'It's not fair', 'I won't stand for that' and soon the fever takes over. Do you suffer from the fevers of jealousy or self pity – perhaps that is one of the most common there is. 'Nobody understands what I have to put up with; everything falls back on me . . . I . . . I . . . I.' And then there is busyness. Have you ever thought of that as a fever? It can be, on those days when the hands on the clock seem to move at twice their normal rate, every job gets interrupted, and you fly round like the White Rabbit muttering, 'I'm late, I'm late, I'm late'.

Now fevers, if left untreated, can quickly progress to something more serious, so don't neglect them. What is the cure? No convenient bottle of medicine to keep on the shelf, but something even more effective.

'Now Simon's mother-in-law lay sick with a fever . . . and he (Jesus) came and took her by the hand and lifted her up, and the fever left her' (Mark 1.30). In the case of Simon's mother-in-law it was a physical fever. But the touch of Jesus is just as effective on fevers of the spirit. So when you feel a fever coming on, stop, and stretch out your hand to Jesus as you bring it to Him in prayer.

Prevention is even better than cure, so let's think about some practical steps that we can take, in partnership with the Holy Spirit, to stop these fevers coming on.

First there is the ordering of your days. You hate to be bound to a timetable, feel it shackles you to a dull routine? Fair enough, but we all know how quickly the minutes turn into hours, and the hours to days and weeks, and without some effort on our part to regulate our use of time, the really vital things get squeezed out.

Unless you are, by nature, a very methodical sort of person, you will probably find it a help to make a rough programme for your day, and an even rougher one for your week. This does not mean that you are rigidly bound by a piece of paper to do the washing on Monday, even if it is pouring with rain, and your shopping on Wednesday even if you have been invited out to tea. But it does help you to dovetail the various jobs together and sort out your priorities.

The first priority is to find a time that you can spend with God. No matter how busy we are, unless we keep in touch with headquarters, neither we nor our homes will grow and develop in the way that He wants, and every other aspect of our lives will be the poorer.

Then there are the ordinary household jobs that are always with us. Can you find a way of doing them more efficiently? Can you cut out some of those visits to the shops by planning several days' meals in advance and shopping accordingly? Have you got the will-power to discipline yourself and your family to tidy up as they go – it's an uphill struggle but pays dividends in the long run.

Having made some attempt to get your 'daily work' under control, can you be free enough from pressure really to listen to your children when they come home from school, and have some time in the day when your toddler can proceed at his own pace, without a constant stream of 'Hurry, hurry, hurry!' from you? And what about some time for you to rest and relax? Everyone should have one period in the day which is their own time, to do their own thing. You may have to cut down things that are good in themselves in order to fit it in, but don't feel guilty. It is almost impossible to have a 'calm and gentle spirit' if you are exhausted because you never stop from morning till night. And often the time to stop is when the pressure is at its peak. Even ten minutes flopped into a chair or onto the bed, consciously relaxing those tensed up muscles and emptying your mind of those racing thoughts, will pay dividends. You don't believe it? Try it and you will be amazed at the result.

So plan your work, and work your plan, remembering that you share the yoke with Jesus and His yoke is easy and His burden light. Get into the habit of praying over problems as they arise, disciplining yourself to face one day at a time, and refusing to let tomorrow's problems cloud today. As Paul says 'And now, just as you trusted Christ to save you, trust Him, too, for each day's problems; live in vital union with Him' (Colossians 2.6, Living Bible).

'This is the day which the Lord has made; let us rejoice and be glad in it' (Psalm 118.24). Today is unique in its opportunities, both to give and to get. This includes days when the going is easy, and days when everything seems too difficult for words. But each day can be faced in this spirit – 'If the Lord has allowed this I *will* be glad' – an act of will and not of emotion.

1 Thessalonians 5.18 puts it another way. 'Give thanks in all circumstances; for this is the will of God in Christ Jesus for you.'

This, above all else, is the best preventative for spiritual fever that I know. And notice that, once again, it is a command and not an optional extra. You have missed the bus? Give thanks; perhaps the Lord has someone He wants you to meet as you wait at the bus stop or walk home. You can't go to that church service? Perhaps tonight will be the night that you can talk to your husband about Jesus?

Does this sound rather idealistic, almost, you might say, unrealistic? Well, do you believe that 'in everything God works for good with those who love him' (Romans 8.28)? In *everything*? If you do, to give thanks in everything is totally realistic. And what is more, it sets you free from the kicking against circumstances and the fretting that so easily take over, to live life at home with that 'gentle and quiet spirit, which in God's sight is very precious'.

Do you sometimes sing with real longing, 'Take from our lives the strain and stress, and let our ordered lives confess the beauty of thy peace'? Well, it is not just a beautiful dream but a practical proposition, and God is waiting to do it – will you let Him?

10 *Bridge over troubled water*

We hear a lot about the communication problem these days. Teenagers cannot communicate with their parents; in-laws lose touch with their married children, and even within the closest relationship of all we hear,

'Bill and I have nothing to say to each other these days. We're just two people living in the same house.'

Only last week, yet another marriage reached the divorce courts for this very reason – the husband could not or would not talk to his wife.

What does this word 'communicate' mean? The Concise Oxford Dictionary defines it like this: 'To impart, transmit (feeling, news, a discovery) to share with, receive, hold intercourse with'. All this sounds simple enough on the surface, so why is it that so many people find it very hard, if not impossible, to share their thoughts and feelings with each other, on any more than a very superficial level? Whatever the reasons, this inability to communicate is the rock on which very many relationships founder, and is a danger which needs to be faced and overcome.

Is it possible for 'two to become one', which according to the Bible is God's plan for marriage? Yes, 'with God all things are possible', as Jesus said in Matthew 19.26, but there is no such thing as 'instant togetherness' to be put on with the wedding ring. People grow together as they learn to know each other, and share experiences over the months and years of marriage. And in addition to getting to know each other, you get to know yourself. How well did you know yourself before you became a wife and mother? Carol did not know that she had a temper until she had three children under two, who had the unfortunate habit of crying in chorus at the most inconvenient moments! Margaret had no idea how much untidiness bothered her until she discovered that Jim just dropped his clothes as he took them off – and left them where they fell!

So the marriage service sets both couples and individuals off on a voyage of discovery, which may go on all through our lives, but all too often stops short because we are afraid. Afraid? Yes, afraid that if we reveal too much, we are handing someone else the weapon with which to hurt us in our most sensitive spot. So, consciously or unconsciously we hold back something of ourselves, in order to have a place of retreat where no one can hurt us. And while we are doing this, true oneness is spoiled to a greater or lesser degree.

Is there a remedy? Yes, if we are willing to consider ourselves dead to the pride that insists that we keep up that protective pretence. When you say with St Paul, 'I am crucified with Christ' you agree, among other things, to be crucified to all forms of pretence. You can be your true self with Jesus because He loves and accepts you as you are. And as the light of His love shows you your faults, and enables you to begin to put them right, so you can learn to accept yourself and to be open with others, giving love with no self-seeking, and no withdrawal because of hurt.

Ask Jesus to give you His love in this way. Communication is essentially a two sided affair, but if even one of the people involved is ready to take this first step into the light, then the vicious spiral of 'I won't . . . because he won't . . . because I won't . . . ' is broken, and you will be ready to take the practical steps that help to bring about a measure of real communication within your family situation.

Every marriage has a language of its own, which is not dependent upon words alone. A glance across a crowded room at a party can say, 'This is fun isn't it?' or 'There's going to be trouble when we get home'. The icy silence in which many couples retire to bed after an argument can carry on the battle just as viciously as any words. A squeeze of the fingers as you wait at the hospital says all that is needed; a cheerful wave and a smile spells out, 'Have a good day'.

And actions say things too. What is the message that comes across from the wife who only has time for what *she* wants to do, goes out in the evening more often than she stays in, and consults her mother over every marital problem?

On the other hand, what are you saying when you substitute an evening at home for an evening out, because he is extra tired and has a cold coming on? Or when you cook his favourite meal, or cheerfully switch over to 'Match of the Day' instead of your favourite serial?

Above and beyond all this, is the most basic and important unspoken communication between husband and wife – the act of making love. Here, as in every other aspect of marriage, willingness to adapt to one another's needs is essential. The fact that two people are married is no guarantee that their need to express their love in physical terms will be the same, and in any case, this can vary in different circumstances. Worry, unhappiness, illness and sheer physical fatigue, can all affect a wife's responsiveness and the same is true for her husband. These will usually sort themselves out, given time, but if they do not, or if the lack of physical harmony is due to deeper problems – resentment, misinformation during childhood, fear of pregnancy or simply lack of knowledge – don't be afraid to ask for help.

Does it seem strange to suggest that you should pray about any problems that you may have in this sphere? God is interested in every aspect of your marriage, and He can give you insight into the cause of your difficulties as well as the grace to put them right. Sometimes the answer is easily found. Perhaps your problem is constant tiredness – you fall asleep as soon as your head touches the pillow with monotonous regularity. If there is no apparent reason for this tiredness, have a chat with your doctor – it may be something as simple as mild anaemia that a course of iron tablets would put right. And if you know that you are simply doing too much . . . recognize the importance of this aspect of your marriage and take steps to cut out something in your daily routine so that you can get some rest.

Jenny was concerned because lovemaking had settled down to being a very routine affair between herself and Paul. She prayed about it, and a few days later found a most helpful book on marriage in her public library, lodged, rather unexpectedly, between two books on theology in the philosophy section! She took it home; she and her husband both read it, and she returned it to the library. She has never seen it there since. A mere coincidence? Perhaps! Certainly the reading of a book did not, in itself, transform this area of their marriage, but the recognition of the existence of a problem and the taking of practical steps to solve it made a great difference.

Mary's problem went deeper than boredom. She deeply resented her husband's refusal to take her Christian faith seriously, and, almost without realizing it, was seeking to punish him by refusing to respond to his lovemaking. A talk with a Christian doctor helped her to face up to the problem, and, after a long inner struggle, to confess it and ask for forgiveness.

Maybe none of these things fit your situation but you are disappointed because you have not experienced the ecstatic feelings portrayed as essential in some marriage manuals. Whatever the cause, this piece of advice can transform your attitude and with it the problems.

'Put your own needs on one side, and concentrate on *giving* love, and satisfying your partner. As you forget yourself and your feelings, you will find that you are able to receive as well.'

Sounds too simple? We have thought about it before – the self-giving love of Jesus. Ask Him for it in this situation and prove for yourself what a difference His love can make.

However vital 'doing' as well as 'saying' may be, there comes a time when there is no substitute for words. The art of talking things over is the oil that keeps a marriage running smoothly. But if you want your 'talking' to have the very best results, ask the Holy Spirit to take control of your tongue, for 'talking' in itself can sometimes do more harm than good.

Have you anything to say?

What did *you* contribute to the conversation last night? Do you expect your husband to make up for the fact that he is out of the house all day and you are not, by having a fund of fascinating stories to bring home each evening? Or do you see it as part of your responsibility to contribute to the supper time chat, other than the rising cost of butter and the children's misdeeds? Be selective – don't talk to the point of boredom about your Christian activities, but look for topics that interest you both.

Of course this will mean a deliberate effort on your part to keep up to date with the world around you, perhaps going more than half way to find a mutual hobby or interest that you can share. In your efforts to be a participator, do remember that every conversation needs a talker *and* a listener and that you should take your turn in both roles. And when you listen, give your husband your *full* attention. One gets so used to giving half an ear to the children's chatter and thinking of other things at the same time, that it can become a habit, and a very exasperating habit at that.

How do you say it?

'It's not so much what you do and say, but the way you do and say it.' Have you ever thought that the *way* in which you phrase a remark can make all the difference between harmony and discord? What effect do you think these two remarks would have on your husband?

'What nonsense! I'm *not* always dashing out in the evening. This is only the second time I've been out this week.'

'Do you *really* feel that I am out too much in the evening? Well, how often do you feel is reasonable?'

The first remark sets the scene for a real slanging match; the second invites reasonable discussion in which people's opinions count for something. So when the atmosphere is stormy, phrase your remarks with care, and respect other people's rights to their own opinions – even if you are convinced that they are wrong!

When do you say it?

Have you a sense of timing? Many misunderstandings arise because we choose the wrong time to bring up thorny subjects. Steer away from unpleasant discussion when you are tired, hurried or otherwise under stress. And if your husband comes home tired and needing an especial helping of comfort and consolation, shelve the problems you were planning to discuss, or the meeting that you were planning to attend and turn your attention to his needs.

Are you there when you are needed?

When he wants to talk are you available? Are you prepared to stay up late if necessary to welcome him home from a business trip? Do you put down your library book willingly to listen to what he has to say? And when he tells you something can he be sure that it will go no further? Not even to your prayer group or your Christian friend down the road? Do you make sure that you are at home together often enough to make conversation possible – you do? Then the battle is almost won. Sharing things together is becoming a habit, and that is a very good foundation for real communication.

Supposing he's the strong and silent type?

It is surprising how often the heroes of romantic novels are portrayed as masterful men of few words. Surprising, because living with a man who is a 'doer' rather than a 'sayer' can bring very real complications in its wake, emphasizing as it does a very basic difference between the sexes.

Most women love to talk. They are more ready than men to discuss their feelings and moods, and find it hard to understand that the majority of men, even the talkers, do not indulge in the verbal soul-searching and prolonged discussion of problems that their wives enjoy. So all of us, and especially those with 'strong and silent' husbands, need to ask the Holy Spirit to show us when to speak and when to keep silent. And on the days when these differences in temperamental make-up irritate, forget your grievances and look for the good points in your marriage partner. Think again about the little kindnesses that you take for granted. How long is it since you have said 'thank you' and really meant it?

'Thank you' and 'I love you'. Five words that need saying every day. They help to build an all-weather communication bridge between husband and wife, which God can bless to make the bad times bearable, and the good times glorious.

11 *Going forward together*

'Yes, I'll come to this service of yours, but after to-night I don't want to hear any more about this Christianity business! Enough is enough!'

With these daunting words ringing in her ears, Jenny set off to church for her baptismal service, leaving Paul to follow a little later. Little did she imagine then that that very evening Paul would be among those making their way to the front of the church, as an indication that he, too, wanted to make a fresh start with Jesus Christ. At that time, Jenny had been a Christian for just about two years.

Ann had rather longer to wait. For nine years she had to learn the lessons of faith and patience in God's school of waiting, while Michael's attitude towards her faith swung between bland indifference and downright disapproval. Through all the ups and downs she clung on to the promise of this verse: 'Take delight in the Lord, and He will give you the desires of your heart' (Psalm 37.4).

This was the assurance that had come to her as she prayed, right at the beginning of her Christian life, that Michael would one day share her faith. She believed that that day would come, but it seemed to be slipping further and further into the future, as, far from getting easier, things got harder. Michael's resistance towards Christianity and Ann's involvement in church life seemed to harden, so that when she was asked to help with a Sunday afternoon teenage group Michael would not entertain the idea. This was in spite of the fact that Ann had been a Sunday School teacher in the past with his full approval. At the same time symptoms of an old heart complaint seemed to return, and Michael could neither eat, sleep nor concentrate on his job. Eventually he went to the doctor, only to be told that there was no physical cause for his symptoms.

Ann was wise enough to see in his moodiness and antagonism the underlying spiritual battle, and, although it was very difficult, said little but prayed constantly as the Holy Spirit did His work. For several weeks Michael battled with the pride that refused to admit that he had been wrong, and the fear of what commitment to Jesus Christ would mean to his way of life. At last the need for peace of mind pushed all these other considerations to one side, and, like Paul, Michael handed over the control of his life to Jesus during a church service.

This does not mean, of course, that the Holy Spirit can work only through a church service or after a set period of time. Don D. became a Christian just one month after his wife, but Mrs A had to wait twenty years, knowing, in the end, that her church regarded her husband as a 'hopeless case', before Bill came to share her faith.

But there are no 'hopeless cases' with God, and whether you are still looking forward to that day when you can walk the Christian pathway with your husband, or are even now taking your first steps together, you can trust Him all the way. Of course, it will make a difference, a wonderful difference to your life which will need adjustments, so let's see how you can best adapt to the changes that this longed-for event will surely bring.

Think back to your own beginnings

Do you remember how you felt, when you started out as a Christian? Were you a bit bewildered, needing to think things out quietly; uncertain of what to read in the Bible or how to pray? Did you long for books to read that would explain those things that you could not understand? Do you remember the time when much that you take for granted now, was all new, exciting and perhaps a little strange?

This is where your husband stands now, and in your enthusiasm to share what you have learned, beware of swamping him with a second-hand faith. Offer advice and help only when it is asked for; be ready to share books that have helped you, but be selective. Match the books you offer to his needs – a book on prayer, for instance, written by a man, with examples from his day to day life, would probably mean more to your husband than the 'prayers from the kitchen sink' that have spoken to your heart so often.

Remember that God deals with us as individuals, so don't fall into the trap of comparing your husband's experience with your own. *You* wanted to sing hymns from morning till night when you were a new Christian? Splendid, but if your husband does not, that is fine too. *He* wants to tell everyone he meets about the wonderful change in his life? Be glad about that, but don't feel guilty because even now you find it difficult to talk to people about your faith. God can meet your needs in this direction, just as He will meet your husband's need in another direction. The important thing is that you both recognize your own needs and bring them to God. You won't become perfect overnight and neither will your husband, so don't try to model your lives on each other, but be ready to help one another, in every way that you can, to become more and more like Jesus.

Pray and read the Bible together

This is not a substitute for your own individual time with Jesus, but a wonderful bonus; a time in which the Holy Spirit can teach you together, and open up a whole new area of communication, as you learn to be open with each other and with Him.

There is an emphasis here on learning – it does not happen all at once. Remember that as a new Christian your husband may find some parts of the Bible easier to follow, and more applicable to his present experience than others. So start off with a gospel like St John or St Mark for your joint reading, rather than your favourite minor prophet. You may prefer to use a book like Daily Light, which has a selection of related verses for each day of the year. And when it comes to discussing it afterwards, don't expect to have all the answers. The Holy Spirit may well reveal something to your husband that you have never noticed – so be prepared to learn from God's Word together.

Praying aloud is one hurdle that some Christians take in their stride, while others never attempt it. Both Ann and Michael felt that God was prompting them to pray together and yet they found it impossible to do so. Michael felt self-conscious at the thought of voicing a prayer that might not 'sound right'. Ann found herself completely tongue-tied when it came to praying aloud with the one person who knew her best in the world – although she had often prayed with her friends.

This situation might have gone on for months had they not mentioned their difficulty to their minister. He visited them in their home, and having talked to them about the various aspects of prayer, suggested that they should pray together before he left.

'I'll pray first, then you Michael, and Ann can round things off for us.'

Those first prayers were very faltering and short. They were not full of long words or holy language, but they were sincere, God heard them, and as they came to Him for help the barrier was broken down. Since then, Ann and Michael have prayed together every day, and they are gradually learning to bring everything, even their own faults and failings, together, to God in prayer.

Do you still feel that this could not work in your situation? That it is too difficult for two shy people like you? God can iron out these difficulties if you are willing to ask Him, and then to do what He tells you. So if you have never started to pray together, ask the Holy Spirit to put the desire to do so into both your heart and your husband's, and then move on from there as He makes the opportunity.

Even when that is accomplished don't expect praying together to be easy, always, even when you have been doing it for years. Sometimes a resentment or a grudge has to be sorted out, or a difference of opinion made up before you can pray at all – for if you are decidedly cross with someone, or not speaking to him at all, you certainly cannot pray with him! The devil may discourage you by seeing to it that your prayer time is interrupted by the telephone or the baby crying; often you may be too tired to 'feel like praying', but persevere nonetheless. Real open-hearted prayer can cement the bonds of a marriage in a way that nothing else can do, so give it the place in your life together that God wants it to have.

Throw away your blue-print for a Christian husband

In your day dreams of the wonderful day when your husband shared your faith, did you build up a glowing picture of exactly how he would behave – based on all your favourite characteristics of the Christian men you knew?

Did you think that he would have the biblical knowledge of David, lead family prayers like Roger, preach like Tony, be the first to put his hand in his pocket for church needs like John, and never miss a service like Peter? You did – with a great many other things beside? Then throw away that blue-print quickly, before you are tempted to try and force the man into the mould, and make one of the biggest mistakes of your life. Praise God for the man He has linked your life with – just as he is. In God's own time He may call your husband to preach, or take a leading part in church affairs, but first he has to grow as a Christian, and he will grow according to God's pattern, not yours.

And people are like plants; they all have their individual growth rates, and no amount of anxious watching over them will make them grow faster than that. Of course, you will want to consider together how you should give to God's work, but give your husband time to learn about the principle of tithing, before you wave a 'deed of covenant' under his nose. Encourage him to take his place in the family of the church, but don't try to rush him into church membership before he feels that he is ready, or into church work, before he has found his own feet as a Christian.

On the other hand, avoid being over-protective, shielding him from the pressures that God intends should help him to grow. There is no need for you to cluck round him anxiously like a hen with one chick. 'Oh no, I don't think you should ask Ben to read the lesson this evening – he's never read the Bible in public before.'

Does that really matter? There's a first time for everyone! Maybe this is not the time for Ben to make a start, but throw away the cotton wool and let him decide for himself when the Holy Spirit is leading him on to do something new.

But perhaps it's in family affairs that you will have to learn to 'let go and let God'. Remember that, although your husband may be a new Christian, in God's ordering of things he is still the leader in your marriage and has the responsibility for ordering the spiritual affairs of the home. So keep your hands off those reins and let him lead, however hesitant he may be at first.

Pray about these matters with him, of course; give advice if it is asked for, and then as he takes each new step be generous in praise, encouragement and, most of all, in prayer.

So don't chivvy, criticise or cosset your husband, but pray for him constantly, confident that the God who has called you both to Himself will lead you on: 'To understand what He wants you to do, and to make you wise about spiritual things, that the way you live will always please the Lord and honour Him, that you will always be doing good kind things for others, all the time learning to know God better and better . . . praying too, that you will be filled with His mighty, glorious strength, so that you can keep going no matter what happens – always full of the joy of the Lord, and always thankful to the Father, who has made us fit to share all the wonderful things that belong to those who live in the kingdom of light' (Colossians 1.9–12, Living Bible).

Some other books to read

Chapter 1

My God is Real – David C. K. Watson (Falcon)
Man Alive – Michael Green (IVP)
Runaway World – Michael Green (IVP)
Journey into Life – Norman Warren (Falcon)

Chapter 2

The Way – Godfrey Robinson & Stephen Winward (Scripture Union)
The Man from Outside – Gordon Bridger (IVP)
The Way Ahead – Norman Warren (Falcon)
What Now? – David Winter (Scripture Union)
I've Got to Talk to Somebody God – Majorie Holmes (Hodder & Stoughton)
Bible Reading Notes from Scripture Union, 5 Wigmore Street, London, W.1

Chapter 3

How to Give Away Your Faith – Paul E. Little (IVP)

Chapter 4

Who Moved the Stone? – Frank Morrison (Faber)
Christian View of Science and Scripture – B. Ramm (Paternoster Press)

For parents:
The Growing Years – Helen R. Lee (Falcon)
The Troubled Years – Helen R. Lee (Falcon)

Teaching for young children:
Simon & Sarah books 1–12 – Scripture Union
Leading Little Ones to God – Marian M. Schoolland (Banner of Truth Trust)

Chapters 5–10

Beyond Ourselves – Catherine Marshall (Hodder & Stoughton)
God's Freedom Fighters – David Watson (MWE)

Chapter 11

Family Life – Martin Parsons (Falcon)

Acknowledgements

This book is not the work of one person, but is based on the shared experiences of women up and down the country. The stories are about real people and are founded on fact, although names and details have been changed to spare them any embarrassment.

So many people have helped with this book. Some have prayed; others have shared in letters, tapes and telephone calls what God has taught them; a few have met in my home to discuss it chapter by chapter.

Three people have played a special part: my mother, who ran the house for a week when it seemed as if the last few chapters would never be written; Janet, who not only typed and re-typed the manuscript, but also offered lots of wise advice and constructive criticism; and finally my husband. He gave me the man's-eye-view of many of the topics covered by the book, and cheerfully weathered the storms of authorship.

To each and every one of them I want to say 'Thank you. Your help made the whole project possible.'

Marion Stroud